# Whistling Past the Tavern

poems by
Jeff Wolverton
Bob Jaeger

All rights reserved
© Jeff Wolverton and Bob Jaeger, 2018

Cover art, a pastel by Nancy Bohm, "The King's Falcon is Your Soul," used with her permission.

Book layout Karl Moeller

ISBN 978-0-692-11608-1

2018

# FOREWORD

Jeff Wolverton and Bob Jaeger, longtime friends of mine in Baba's companionship, have brought a wonderful new approach to presenting poetry—they have formed a sort of literary "duet," Jeff on saxophone, Bob on bass, then Jeff playing the piano and Bob the xylophone. Their themes vary and merge, soar into the heavens and skim the surface of life, all, however, beginning and ending within the Oceanic Being of Avatar Meher Baba.

Bob and Jeff have written modern poetry here—not the sonnets of Shakespeare or the ghazals of Hafiz—but do not let the contemporary formats distract you from finding the substance within. If they were enlightened I would be reminded of translations I've seen of Rumi, but alas, they are not enlightened, not yet, and so I must content myself with being reminded of T.S. Eliot and Pablo Neruda. Because they are poems inspired by the Divine Beloved, however, these are soul songs, never poetry just to be poetry but poetry to seek His company and refresh it. They are rewarding, perhaps, to the same degree that the reader shares that longing.

This small volume brings a glimpse of Baba's future. Poetry will reign in the New Humanity, as more and more people strive to seek the Beloved's company and share it. New styles and forms will pour forth as the lover experiments with different ways to tempt the Beloved into taking residence in his heart, and life will be richer, truer, infused with the Love-streams that flow forth from the Ocean of His Love. Enjoy these early exercises presented here, exercises in calling forth and listening to the Word behind all words.

Rick M. Chapman
11 May 2018

PREFACE

"The energy which is expended in mere thinking, talking or writing is like the steam which escapes through the whistle of the railway engine. The whistle makes a noise, and is even interesting, but it cannot drive the engine. No amount of whistling can move the engine forward. The steam has to be harnessed and used intelligently in order that it may actually take the engine to its destination. That is why the sages have always insisted on practice rather than theory. This applies particularly to those who want to know and realize God."*

Meher Baba

Eruch, one of Baba's intimate companions, used to say about Meherazad (much to the horror of some), "You come here to die, to be effaced in the Beloved, to dissolve in His arms." And another companion, Darwin Shaw, always with an enigmatic smile on his face would often say, "Sooner or later you discover you're nobody, and that is not an unhappy discovery."

...Which brings us to the practice Baba recommended most often. He was clear that for some span of time after leaving His body, the path of love remains wide open if only we can follow the deepest promptings of the heart.

Baba never said it would be easy, but as Baba's sister Mani explained, "The road of the mind is narrow, and for a dnyani (seeker) it is a long journey. The road of the heart, however, has no limits and it's the most direct to God. For the dnyani there are a thousand questions to all of which the bhakti (lover) has one answer, and it is all-sufficient and satisfying." **

And that is our Beloved.

The Lane of Love, then, seems to be a direct route to the inner Tavern. Once we sniff it out and begin to follow the scent, we will never be lost until, at last—Wine!

A toast to the Boss! We hope these whistlings past the drunken Tavern are more than just unharnessed steam, that they attract Your keen attention and entertain Your lovers.

Jeff and Bob

---

*Naosherwan Anzar, ed., Meher Baba's Spiritual Parables, (A Glow Publication, Dehra Dun, 1967) p. 9
**Jimmy Mistry, ed., Letters From The Mandali, Vol. 2 (AMBPPCT, 1983), p. 73

## A Great Need

Out
Of a great need
We are all holding hands
And climbing.
Not loving is a letting go.
Listen,
The terrain around here
Is
Far too
Dangerous
For
That.*

*Daniel Ladinsky, *The Gift*, Poems by Hafiz
(Penguin Compass: NY, 1999) p. 165
—used by permission

Dedicated to the True Friend
in gratitude for the many
dear friends in His Love
He has placed in our lives.

*Where Does He Reside?*

The hourglass must be broken
before one is released
into sacred time.

You ask what I'm doing?
I'm listening for the precious sound
of His footsteps echoing
down the winding corridor
of this eternal moment.

*JW*

*All I Want*

In this silent morning as
Light pours through old glass
Rippling over the golden wall.
Afternoon, walking the dog
As clouds roll, snow begins,
Leaves startle in bitter winds.
Evening, all done and undone,
Weariness pools, leaks in
As day grows pale and thin.
All I want is You, for a moment,
A touch, a glance across the dark,
Only a spark of Your lovely light before
Giving me up to the fast falling night.

*BJ*

## An Artist's Fate

A heavy cloud passes
across my heart's sky today.
I can't help thinking how cheated we are by life—
it continually destroys yesterday
and all its beauty,
leaving behind only an empty memory
we can't touch or taste.

Why have You set it up this way?
All those magnificent times we poured
our souls into—gone!
What if an artist, in order to create
a new landscape, had to paint over
his previous canvas!

You reply knowingly,
"How will you ever step into the being
of God who was not created,
as long as you drag around with you
all your creations—past, present and future?

*JW*

*Sitting in the Barn*

Sitting in the barn
Pulling pages from the journal.
Whose life was this anyway?
Too bad we cannot as easily
Rip out those dim pages of mind
Filled with preference and expectation,
Written over again and again,
A sanskaric palimpsest
The mind gazes through
Even when we try
To remember You.

*BJ*

*Go With the Current*

The Beloved has said,
"Don't despair. Though the waves
of world affairs are fierce and choppy,
look to the steady current
beneath them.
It is bearing all of us
to a hidden luminous sea within.
Pull up the anchor of where you are stuck
and allow yourself to be carried away
by this divine gulf stream.

Saint and sinner, both, can be the benefactors
of a free ride from the tremendous pull
coming from the inner ocean of divinity.
In that realm, losing your moorings is a sure sign
that you're finding your way."

*JW*

*On the Ocean of Love*

You have told us
Somewhere deep lies
A pearl of great price
And all we need do
Is dive.

Dear Baba,
I might try that
Were I not chained
To the boat.

But here I am
Where You have put me,
Storm tossed and calm
Rowing and resting.

You are the keel and rudder,
The oars and shoulders,
The hands, the hearts.

Oh Beloved,
Be our North Star.
For here we all are
In the same leaky boat
Rowing mightily,
Going where?
Bailing furiously,
To keep out what?

*BJ*

*Boat or Marina?*

The spiritual journey is not about
steering our little boat safely
through a busy marina,
without bumping into anything.
We have to become
the entire marina itself.

Spirituality is not about going somewhere,
but about expansion of being,
so that little by little everything
in creation finds its loving place
in our heart.

*JW*

*Reason or Rhyme?*

Shall I do this, shall I do that,
Take off my coat, put on my hat,
Take the dog for a morning walk,
Invite You in for a little talk?
You are not here, You are not there,
I cannot find You anywhere,
And mind wanders far and loose
Recalling lines from Dr. Seuss.
All I want is a glimpse of You,
But the endless drivel of don't and do
Distracts and leads me down the path
Of ruing this or planning that,
Thinking just get up and go,
But shoulds and coulds are all I know.
Yet nowhere I can think to be,
Nothing at all I wish to see,
Nothing I would hold more dear
Than a moment with You, here
Beloved, without and within.
Help me open, invite You in,
Have You near, and have You far,
However You wish, wherever You are.
Though I wander from reason to rhyme
Through this and that and drifting time,
The endless tide, the in and out,
The here and there and roundabout,
The up and down, the joy, the fear,
Please, Beloved, be near. Be near.

BJ

*Feeling Crushed*

When there is so much heartache
in this life with You,
how can I encourage anyone
to run after You?

Can I honestly ask someone
to endure the weight of mountains
on the flimsy promise that they
will one day be crushed into
diamonds?

What do I have to show
as guarantee that the pain
will be worth it,
I who still carry around
worthless stones in my jacket
pockets?

*JW*

*Tug-of-War in Toka, 1928*

They all wanted Baba's company,
So they had a tug-of-war.
Holding His wrists, they pulled,
The ashram boys on one side,
The Meherabad girls on the other.
Baba said, "Pull with all your might.
Let's see who is stronger
And who loves me more."

And now You're gone,
These few years that
Seem so many,
And we can only wonder
How to hold, Beloved,
How to pull You close.

*BJ*

*Hanging by a Thread*

Today life flows smoothly,
but at any moment my selfish desires
could pound at the door,
like a police raid in the night.

My fate hangs precariously
by a thread held in Your hand –
that I move toward the light
is my soul's response
to Your loving eyes,
hidden within the timeless veils
of this moment.

*JW*

*That Narrow Place*

Silent winter sky gray
Above and all around.
Even the birds are quiet.

Still pool on the path
Reflects trees
Clear in every detail,

So real I imagine
I might slip between
That mirror and
This, into a place
Closer than the space
Between hands at prayer,
To find You at last,
Beloved.

BJ

*Home Sweet Home*

Beware the repetition
of the Beloved's name in the heart!
It acts like an infestation of termites
that eventually eats you
out of house and home,
until you are forced to flee
your very lodgings and become
one of those illustrious residents
inhabiting the entire universe.

*JW*

*Call the Guards*

My neighbor installed an alarm
That alerts the local police should
Thieves break in to steal his stuff.
He pays a monthly fee for this.
I would pay, and handsomely,
For a service alerting me
When that old burglar Maya
Distracts, waving some bright
Bauble while sneaking in,
Intent on prying from my grasp
The priceless treasure of Your name.

*BJ*

*Blessed Occupant*

This morning You entered
my house, occupying all the rooms,
leaving no room for me.
I am blessed. Even saying "me"
is a mistake and can easily
break this magic spell.
For a few precious moments,
I cannot return home.
I have the unspeakable privilege
of witnessing You
as the sole occupant
of all the rooms of myself.

*JW*


*Just Out of Sight*

Old dog barks a warning.
I open the door to look, and in the street
The red fox stops and gazes back
For a long moment, then glides away
Under trees white and weighed down.
You touch my heart, slip away too,
Leave me longing for a glimpse.

*BJ*

*The Darkness Seeks The Light*

When Light enters this world,
the darkness rushes up to meet it.
Those who are loving and kind—
don't be disheartened when you encounter
greed and selfishness along your path.
It is darkness' way of paying tribute
to the majesty of love.

Look what happened to Jesus—
He traveled on foot through
Galilee, filling desolate hearts
with His benevolence and grace for free,
and yet darkness
was ever at His heels.
Mohammed, too, was persecuted
and hunted throughout the Arabian Peninsula,
and who was more loving and just than He?

Darkness seeks the Light to be transformed.
When you feel darkness around you,
light must be somewhere close by—
a hidden saint who might hand you something
ordinary across a counter,
that contains a precious seed
of love which takes root in your being;

or perhaps the invisible wake
of a simple work, done
in a spirit of sacredness by someone
you have never met, could carry to you
a blessed life raft;
or maybe even your own
pure momentary intention
never to harm yourself or another
is enough to bring a little light
into the darkness.

*JW*

*A Day in January*

We walk, old red dog and I,
along this day of unexpected
warmth and gurgling melt.
Her belly drips from slop the
short legs kick, and I push
back the hat, shoulder the jacket.

The way we go is quiet, the day fine
until shadow brings a sudden chill
and the old familiar emptiness.

We return tired, and I towel her dry.
She naps while I sip coffee, consider
imagined past, imagined future,
fleeting and no less imagined now.

Yes, a fine day for walking—
but where are You who claim
to be everywhere and in everything,
deeper than breath, closer to
heart than pumping blood?

You have shown the limitation
of thought, the futility of action
without deep knowledge, deeper love.

What now?

Forgive me, Beloved.
I do not have the old dog's patience,
and it seems just now, on this aimless
day in January, there is nothing left
but the waiting.

*BJ*

*28 October 2008*

Hours before dawn,
under the vast canopy of stars,
I set out for Your Tomb
across the grassy fields.
The night cool, damp,
all around the incessant buzz
of crickets,
the sound of devotional music
from the distant village,
a lone truck rumbling
along the road miles away.
In the air along the way,
a faint scent of flowering shrubs
held in the moist air.
I hear the sound of my own footsteps
on the gravel path—
all these sensations, so fresh and clear,
echo Your exquisite presence
right here with me.

*JW*

## A Moonless Indian Night

One night late at Viloo Villa, sleepless I crept through the quiet house, out the front door, across the courtyard and down the road into darkness. I sat on a low wall in that starry vastness and watched as water buffalo and carts with swaying lanterns and people passed, walking and riding, coming and going. They stared, and under the moonless sky unfettered by street lights in that timeless space, a place so alien I neither belonged nor did not belong, mind finally pushed forth a trickle of nervousness, and I went back down the road, in to bed and to sleep. For years I thought it all simply whim on my part, but I know You gave that moonless Indian night, and ever since have planted me here and there and in this now where some current of not belonging persists and often surges up a want of not wanting to belong to any place, but only to You, Beloved Lord.

BJ

*God's Fools*

The Beloved's scissors do not cut
along the dotted lines of convention—
He cuts lives to shreds
and scatters them to the winds.
His true lovers have no address in this world,
though they can be found here,
and sometimes there.

They have been stripped of moods,
and wander in a succession of states
that have no past or future.

When they appear to be plunged
in grief, don't say they have lost something—
they weep for what they cannot find.
And when they dance in ecstasy,
don't say they have found things you value—
they are mighty rivers rejoicing
as they meet the sea.

*JW*

*The Wish*

I wanted to open the heart's door,
enter that raucous tavern where You
fill the glasses of all those drunkards
who have given in and given
completely up, even if I could only
watch from a quiet corner at the back.
Instead I stumbled into the echoing
cavern of thought where hardened
growths of memory and crystals
of desire glint with empty promise.
But then a crack, a small warm ray,
the sure knowledge that only
Your wish truly satisfies.

BJ

*Nothing to Offer*

I am not the mystic's water pitcher,
capsized in the ocean, so sunk
in fullness that it won't pour.

Today my vessel is so thick with wanting
that nothing will flow
out of its spout—not a drop
to offer the thirsty river of creation.

JW

*Walking the Dog*

Short lead or long makes no difference.
He is always at the bitter end,
Straining after the next bird or squirrel
Or trace of those who passed before.
If I try to change the route
Or simply slow down to consider,
To meet these moments on my terms,
He jerks me straight,
Pulls me back to his pressing needs.
I am mostly patient with him.
He makes my arm strong
And reminds me how the mind works,
How the ravenous dogs of desire
And worry, of anger and fear drag me
Across the rough edges of the world
No matter how I wish to sit,
Or set my course, or set my heart.

BJ

*What's All the Racket?*

This world is like the rowdy neighbors
upstairs, partying all night.
The more you complain,
the more stubborn they become,
and the stomping of feet
and blaring music goes on.

It is our fated, God-awful career
to learn to live with the whole wide range
of raucous noise, until one day
we sink beneath the warm waves
of His silence.

*JW*

*Meditation*

Arriving at the Center,
Moist breeze stirs
The hundred shades of green.
Sweat trickles, scalp itches.
Shall I go for a walk, swim,
What if I run short of food,
Coffee, clean underwear,
Will I find a ride to the store?
Beloved Baba, here I am—
Not quite alone.

BJ

*Left Holding the Baggage*

Just relax. Do you still doubt
that our Beloved accepts you
and is carrying you to the goal?

Dear friend, you're like a man
standing in the aisle
of a moving train car,
holding his suitcases—
thinking he's still waiting
for the train
on the station platform.

*JW*

*Joyriding with Monkey Mind*

Winter sun touches the porch,
and I open the door just a crack
so the old red dog and I can
peer up and down the quiet street,
then slip together into the cold day.
I'm determined to remember You,
walk with You, carry You
in my heart no matter what.
But then, not three steps out,
bass thumping, treble screaming
Maya rushes by in a red pickup
truck and carries me careening
through another average day with
that distracted madcap at the wheel.
Hours later at the grocery store,
in a quiet moment between Asian
and Mexican, I remember You again
just as someone talking on the phone
drops a jar of salsa, and off we ride.

BJ

*Too Much to Carry*

All my needs I've packed
in one small suitcase.
For my wants,
I've rented a warehouse.

*JW*


*A Prayer for Grace*
    *while waiting at the airport*

"Attention passengers—
Do not leave your baggage unattended.
Unattended baggage may be confiscated
And may be destroyed."

Baggage?
I would leave it all in a heap
On this hard plastic seat and beg,
Please confiscate and destroy as you wish.
I would dance through your gate laughing,
And so much lighter with only my luggage.

*BJ*

*Bad Day for Fishing*

Today my thoughts and emotions
are all tangled up like fishing lines–
I cannot produce one single line
to cast out and catch You
in the vast sea of this moment
and reel You in.

*JW*


*Boathouse Haiku*

Far off thunder grumbles
Frogs across Long Lake answer
Baba, Baba

*BJ*

*Greater Than Darkness*

When you find yourself trapped
in the darkest subterranean
cavern of your mind,
in that painful place, pause and listen—
there is a faint voice that won't be silenced,
telling you that all this is not real.

In that darkness, wait for the sure lamp
carried by your soul, even if that wait
seems endless, because you are
in essence God, and that tiny lamp,
a spark of the divine,
is greater than all darkness.

JW

*Just Enough*

I begged a glance
But glimpsed instead chains
Beneath the beckoning warmth
Of everything these eyes can see,
Heard the cold rattle ,
Each link forged in the fire of want
No matter how fleeting.
Oh Beloved, since Your Wish
Alone guides true, grant this fool
The wit, the strength, just sense
Enough to follow only You.

BJ

*Wine Aging in a Glass*

I am only cheap wine
poured into Your crystalline glass.
No matter.
Look how quickly I age in Your upraised hand.
My life, once green and immature,
is now caught in that sacred space
between crystal wineglass
and Your lips.

*JW*

*Adolescent in Your Love*

May I anticipate You more
Than the day's first coffee,
Desire Your company
More than solitude,
Hunger for Your touch
More than all hungers,
For I am adolescent
In Your love.
Here I am nonetheless,
Knowing only muddled love
Dreaming warm caresses,
This sighing love all mixed
With cold and distance.
Oh guide these hands, this heart,
For I am adolescent in Your love.

*BJ*

## A Demolition Job

Sometimes when a house is too old
and broken down, any further repairs
are of no use.
It's better to demolish the structure
completely and start anew.

That's what the Beloved must do
when faced with our outdated egos'
endless need for repairs.
The love He has to give could never fit
into that crude shack of a house anyway.
Only a place that has no walls or roof
can house His boundless soul.

*JW*

*Dance of the Tick*

Imagine the world an immense dog
Splashing about in the Ocean of Love,
And this I a blind tick buried in its hide.
This I, warm and cozy and well fed
Comes to the nagging suspicion
It cannot see and does not really know,
And all this roiling and boiling blood
Somehow no longer satisfies,
So it begs for Your Grace, Beloved.
However, just the merest touch
Of Your incandescence brings such
Screaming fear and hanging on
For dear blind and buried life that
It begs again, this time for Your Mercy.
Why not, dearest, simply relax
And let Him do as He wishes,
As He knows best what you must do
And what you can bear.

BJ

*Fire and Brimstone*

We've all been cornered
by religious fanatics
who try to shove God down our throats—
as if that Great One
could be swallowed through the gullet.

They would terrify us into believing.
But believing in what?
Certainly, our Beloved, who makes His home
in each of us, would not feel comfortable
with a frightened new believer
standing nervously in front of Him.

If you're dying to get
into heaven and terrified of hell, dear one,
you are far, far from your Beloved's
warm and friendly door.

*JW*

*Fool Greets the Missionaries*

One of these glorious summer mornings I will arise early and go out before combing hair or putting in my plastic eye to sit on the porch in my old green robe sipping coffee and humming jaunty songs to You, Beloved. I will open the gate with a flourish and a grin waving prayers and poems with a hearty harhar—I'll read yours, bucko, if you'll read mine—hold up my cup and dance and sing out that God has said He will fill our cups to the brim with His best wine if only we will empty them before knocking on the tavern door.

On second thought, the best course might be simply to greet warmly and remember that You are everywhere and in everything, even in spaces we thought empty, and even those judged most heinous are never damned by You. Anyway, though I know nothing of eternity, I do attend religiously the First Illusory Church of the Daily Puzzle.

*BJ*

*Not Just Yet, Sir*

Every moment, perfect saints
like Hafiz and Rumi
knock on the door of our outer world,
inviting us to join them in the divine realm within.
They come knowingly,
with bogus maps and pictures under their arms,
the kind shown to tourists to entice them
to go to distant places—
anything to lure us to travel
to that jeweled island in the midst
of the inner celestial sea.
But we demur,
saying we have work to do,
more duties to fulfill in this world
before that divine vacation and suggest,
"Come back at the end of my life,
maybe after I've seen
my first great-grandchild."

JW

*Kalahari Rain*

When rain stops,
Rivers shrink to pools,
Then moist patches,
And then to nothing at all.
Wise frogs dive into mud
That soon hardens,
And there each one waits
Alone, hoarding moisture
In the dark, in the silence,
Until the next rain sets it free,
Blinking, drinking again
Through mouth and skin,
Through everything,
This water, this water...

The lesson for us?
Oh Beloved,
Help us remember You
And not too often ask
How long?

*BJ*

*That Place in the Soul*

Here, in this bustling city
at the height of the holiday season,
amid the busy rush of shoppers
and the sound of bells and carols,
I am alone
on some faraway mountaintop
in the clear sunlight
with You.

*JW*


*A Moment*

Quiet snow, a book, and You.
Heart warm and full.
Then foolish mind thinks
How lovely spring will be,
Sitting with You, a book,
And thoughts of winter quiet.

*BJ*

*Clearly Unpalatable*

What kind of Chef is this—
before I'm allowed to dine at His table,
I have to learn how to eat crow!

*JW*


*Swift Kick*

In the orange circle of sweet-sour sauce,
This bright yellow yolk appears festive,
But too generous a dollop on the eggroll
Claws through sinuses to explode
Like napalm behind the eyes until
Sneezing, crying, gasping for breath
All consciousness goes—
No worry, no want, no future or past—
Nothing in the universe matters.
For this fiery fraction of a second,
Free.
Chicken soup for the soul?
Nice enough in its way,
But what the soul really wants
May be more along the lines of
Too much Chinese mustard.

*BJ*

*God by Any Other Name*

When we reach for the best in ourselves,
we're all drawing from the same well,
sending a bucket deep down
into a hidden pool of grace
and pulling up floodwaters
that drown out selfishness.

Why is it so few people see
that this common well is the one God
we all turn to, that we've never drawn our water
from different sources?

JW

*Longing for Light*

The playground overflows with laughter.
As old dog and I pass the schoolyard,
Sun pours from the blue bowl of sky.
A tall chain link fence separates,
Transforms the sidewalk
Into a strange, arabesque passage
Of shifting shape and shadow.
There is no facile segue here, no
Comfortable blend of dark and bright.
The days simply do not satisfy
As they did before this thirst arose
For Your warmth, Your light.

BJ

*Heart in Shadow*

    There is nothing worse
than when I don't feel
              You near;
it's like a fairground
    during the off-season,
a vacant building in the ghetto,
a children's playground,
            during the rain.

*JW*


Morning sun grows
Your face glows
Heart opens

Clouds flow
Your face in shadow
Heart closes.

*BJ*

*Going Out Without a Coat*

One day the Beloved, speaking
metaphorically, said to me,
"You are comfortable when the temperature
is between fifty and eighty degrees.
But now I want you to feel comfortable even
at twenty degrees below and a hundred twenty
above.
If you cannot bear
the full range of temperatures,
how will you ever acquire real poise?"

He was speaking of my heart's tolerance.
How much unpleasantness could I bear
before screaming in protest?
How will I be able to participate
fully in life, if I feel hurt
by the searing heat of an angry glance,
or am threatened by the thin chilling smile
of indifference?

*JW*

*On Returning Home from the Ocean*

Far from Your home on this rainy day,
I find You have kept all the darkness I brought.
I find You have lightened my heart.
What a blessing, what a joke, Beloved.
In honor of Your infinite humor and grace
I will go out into the world today
Without money, without wallet,
Without documentation or proof,
Hoping You will recognize me and laugh.
I will go without notebook and pen
Knowing the only thing worth remembering
Is Your sweet name over and over,
How the rhythm of it modulates my breath,
My step, the swing of arms, the arc of my gaze.
With nothing to talk about and nothing to do,
Nothing to see and no one to meet but You,
I will go out with nothing in my pockets,
And I will even go without glasses.
This will blur the sharp outlines of the world,
But may help me recognize You
Should You suddenly step out of the tavern
And invite this thirsty old complaining fool in.

*BJ*

*Losing Focus*

Many times out of carelessness,
I've dropped bottles of Your rare wine—
pieces of broken glass scattering everywhere,
and the precious contents soaking
into the earth, of no use
to anyone.

This is what happens
when I turn from You to fulfill desire—
my heart is quickly emptied
of its rare substance.

*JW*

*There is This*

Oh Beloved, let me long only for You,
Let go all foolishness this fool would do,
Distracted wandering, turns and twists,
Put all of that aside—there is still this:
Your smiling picture radiant on the wall
As early sun lights up the shadowed hall,
Your quiet touch in this still shrouded heart
Before all the thinking and doing can start.
As weariness grows of old hooks and snares,
Of constantly barking desires and cares,
Allurement of future, dead weight of past,
Please Lord, one desire alone—hold fast.
Refuse old Maya's too familiar lures
And hold but one longing—to be Yours.

BJ

*Looking for Work*

Lightning can set a tree instantly
on fire—this we know.
But who knows what one glance
of Yours can do to the vast continents
of the heart?

What was once for me
a place of satisfaction, You turned
overnight into a land of discontent.
This whole world is now empty,
unless You give me something of love to do.

I've been reduced
to a day laborer on a street corner,
begging for a bit of work.
I now depend on Your generous employment
to sustain me.

JW

*Near and Far*

At the end of the street, on top of the hill,
Blue vastness spreads so far and still.
The silent mountains seem so near,
Though miles lie between there and here.

How is it that You, Beloved, nearer
Than bone and blood, worry and fear
Can seem so far that poor heart cries out
For an end to distance, distraction and doubt.

If only You were near as mountains and sky,
Not banished to terrible distance by
Desires and plans, hopes, selfish schemes,
The endless nothing of dreams into dreams.

I would go anywhere, I know this much,
For just a glance, a smile, a touch.

*BJ*

*Getting Outside Ourselves*

The experience of grace
is not the monopoly of saints.
You and I can feel its warm descent
in the heart,
if for one moment we do something
out of genuine love—
something that causes us
to reach beyond ourselves.

Artists and selfless people sometimes
feel grace moving through them,
a divine current greater than
themselves.
What of the mystics who have drowned
in this overpowering current
and have re-surfaced
as the living source of grace itself!

*JW*

*Saved*

After visiting Your home on the shore,
I have returned to Colorado.
It is a gray and rainy day, and cold.
Left to my own devices
I could dredge worry and old hurt,
Mix in a dash of guilt, some fear,
A little loneliness and just
A pinch of self-indulgent doubt.
It's an old recipe, and I know it by heart,
But You, Beloved, don't even let me start.
The rain is fine for walking in with dogs,
And after that the laundry warms my hands.
The dear wife You dropped into my
Bumbling life will be home later tonight.
I will shop for things I know she likes
And wait for her with a meal much finer
Than the stew You saved me from today.

BJ

*Vulnerability is the Key*

The Beloved says, "Between you and Me
there are forty-nine veils; between Me and you
there are no veils."

But why do You keep me
so many veils away at a distance,
gazing at You, when my heart longs to feel
my cheek next to Yours?
Do You think I'm content with a glimpse of a
glimpse
of a glimpse of You?

For years I've tried to draw close,
sometimes making strenuous spiritual effort,
but still Your precious intimacy eludes my heart.

From deep within me, You answer,
"Dear one, all your strengths and virtues together
will not pierce a single veil.
It is only when I bring up in you
what is most weak and vulnerable
that the veils are loosened and drop away,
so that one day—you just fall
into My arms."

JW

*Pulling at a Thread*

I noticed the thread on the button of the shirt
And pulled, and when the button fell off
There was a moment's irritation until
The thought occurred to me, the possibility
That this unraveling could simply continue
Up the sleeve, across the shoulders, down
The torso and the other arm all at once,
And then by some odd attraction unknown
To science, progress from the shirt tail
To the shorts and trousers and socks,
And then, inexplicably jumping
Like lightning from earth to sky
The mystery would continue from the tips
Of the toes all the way up the body till
Nothing remained to my wife's astonished
Gaze but a slappyhappy Cheshire grin.
Then side to side that too would go,
Not fading cat-like but a clean unwinding,
And then another lightning leap to mind,
And all the dark and hidden residue
Floating up and up like buried stuff
From deep swamp muck stirred by wind
Coming to light and lining up bit by bit
Like the loopy threads on a dog food sack,
And if you can find just the right place to start,
They unzip thread by binding thread,
Quickly and easily, just like that,
Until nothing is left but You, Beloved.

BJ

*Reluctant to Take the Plunge*

There is a bridge we must pass over
before we are united with everyone and
everything.
But on that other side,
no "I" or "we" remains—
That is why I hold back, afraid
to lose myself in You.

I am not one of those reckless moths
circling the candle flame,
oblivious of impending destruction.
For that foolhardiness,
You will have to make me totally drunk
on Your love before I would dive
into the burning flames
of union.

*JW*

*The Trap*

You had been living in the dark
space behind the kitchen cabinets.
I knew because I found your tiny
black turds, first under the sink and then
on a bottom shelf next to a bag of barley,
a small hole chewed in one corner.
I set a shiny plastic trap all enclosed
with a tunnel leading to peanut butter.
It may have tempted but did not catch,
and in the drawer under the oven I saw
the same dark signs of your anxious life.
Then in the cellar I found a spring trap,
old and stained but still deadly quick,
and last night I snapped Your mouse form.
It was swift I think, and though a little sad
I do not ask forgiveness, only turnabout
as I scurry from place to place and wait,
sometimes full but often empty,
always shaking with joy or dread,
fearing, hoping You will spring Your trap
and catch for keeps this trembling heart.

*BJ*

*Don't Settle for the Cheap Seats*

People talk about the battle
between good and evil,
but our Beloved says that all life
is one divine symphony.

Unfortunately, most of us have the cheap seats
next to the percussion section.
And if we had our way, we'd get rid of
those noisy musicians making all the racket.
But that will never do.
What is needed is to pay the price for a better seat,
one in the center of the auditorium,
where the percussion blends in perfectly
with the rest of the orchestra.

The cost of that seat is our life.
That's where the mystics sit.
They don't get all caught up in good and evil.
They sit back and enjoy
the magnificent performance.

*JW*

*Singing at the Tomb*

As song and music swell, sit with knees
Poking into the aisle and see no matter
How the body bends this is still the world
That none of us fit utterly well,
Always awkward, poking at life,
Prodded down or up whatever smooth or
Rocky path we have stumbled onto,
Eyes shut mostly tight against Your light.

How fortunate to poke so gangly
The sharp edges of this world yet know
You not only were, You are,
And here we all somehow are in this life,
In this place with you, Beloved, singing.

BJ

*The Indestructible You*

The world may break in
and ransack my house, leaving it
in shambles,
but it cannot take away
Your presence within me—

no more than a raging storm
can destroy the earth's
precious atmosphere.

*JW*


*Shish Ke-Baba*

With all the excess fat of wants
and desires, and raw meat
that needs to be cooked out of me,
why not just stick me on a rotisserie
and roast me over the raging fire
of Your Tomb,
and from time to time,
ask the person giving out prasad,
who usually has plenty of time
on his hands, to turn me over
until I'm done on all sides,
fit for Your table,
O King of Kings.

*JW*

*Still Waiting*

Squatting in this shabby hovel of self,
Squinting out through the cracks,
Hoping for a glimpse of You,
I wait.
I have no patience, but I have no choice,
For there is no door,
So I wait.
Now and then You fill my heart,
The cracks grow wide, and it seems
For a moment there are no walls at all,
But You go.
And I must wait.
I do the thousand things that must be done,
I do them in bunches or one by one,
And I even forget that I am waiting.
Then I remember,
And I wait.
Yes, yes, I know,
You have explained the law of must
And all about sanskaras and fate,
But I really don't give a tinker's damn.
I'm tired of this hovel and sick of the sham.
There is nothing new.
There is only You.
So I wait.

BJ

*Rattle Your Cage*

It's said that to escape this world prison
requires inside help—God's grace.
It cannot be done on our own.
But how to attract this grace?
The mystics tell us
it is not something that can be achieved
through effort;
it is a spontaneous gift from God.

However, don't be one of those forlorn prisoners
moping in his cell, resigned to fate.
Even though you cannot produce
a drop of grace, you can at least
rattle your prison bars
until you attract
the Warden's attention.

*JW*

*Upper Meherabad, 1937*

You sit astride the white donkey,
Right arm raised high, waving,
Eyes looking into the distance,
And at this distance of years
That is no distance at all,
We realize suddenly
It is a wave not of departure
But of greeting,
And with just a little effort
We can lift up our hearts
And rush to Your side.

*BJ*

*Don't Settle for a "B" Movie*

Ever notice after leaving
a movie theater, if the drama aroused
only your superficial emotions,
how ordinary and even small you feel?
And if it touched your deeper feelings,
how like a prince or princess you stride out?

The saints know this secret
and always absorb themselves
in things that appeal to their heart and soul,
so they live perpetually expansive lives.

JW

*At This Late Date*

It is summer here, Beloved.
If I wait till afternoon for our walk,
The old dog pants, avoids pavement.
We pause in shade of scattered trees
Before setting out again into the glare,
And I entertain passing thoughts of
Dim murmuring taverns and cold beer.
But at this late date I know very well
That only the wine of Your love will do.

BJ

*No One on the Sidelines*

The Beloved once chided me,
"In this divine game of love,
how can you call your love genuine,
which leaves so many standing
on the sidelines?

Anyone who justifies leaving anyone
out of their heart
has not touched even the robe
of Jesus, or caught a glimpse
of the Buddha's compassionate eyes."

*JW*

*Nasik, 1938*

Legs crossed You sit,
A pillow behind Your back.
Chummy the spaniel lies
Alert yet serene,
Golden rump against
Your right knee,
Bringing new meaning
To the old phrase,
You lucky dog.

*BJ*

*Don't Think You're Just a Speck*

The Beloved has said:
"Don't say you are nothing more
than a scrap of paper on the roadside,
blowing in the wind.
Don't be so proud to think you are
that insignificant!
You are also the wind itself,
and infinitely more.

"Don't be one of those who look up at the stars
and feel so small. Those very heavens
are telling you how immense you really are!
Do you think you'd see the stars
if they weren't already in you?"

Our Beloved has said repeatedly:
"When a drop merges in the ocean,
it becomes the ocean itself.
Don't wall yourself off from the universe.
Be a cube of sugar, eager
to dissolve in your morning cup of tea."

*JW*

*Lodged*

Iron falls to rust and flesh to rot,
And all that seems to be is really not.
Hills wash to plains and plains to sea
And where this wrack, this mote, this me?
Lodged here, Lord, and where are You?
'Oh, such a small distance to push through'
You say, yet much too far for me to walk.
Thought spins. Words fall in useless talk.
I'll do as I must and You as You wish,
Though I gasp and writhe, a landed fish.
So pull or push, embrace or shove
Till distance disappears in love.
Of one thing only am I sure—
I am Yours, Beloved, I am yours.

BJ

*Happily Lightweight*

I have two bodies,
one that's ordinary and has weight,
the one we all have, and another that's just
a hollow shell.

Oh, let me be the empty shell,
for through it You can live my life for me,
while I watch quietly from
the windowsill.

*JW*

*Your Hand in My Glove*

This 'I' a tattered glove
Worn so long and now
Old again and worn.

May Your wish be the hand
That clenches and opens,
That works and rests,
And Your love be the blood
That warms the fingers
That move in the glove
Till this job is done
And a new glove is bought.

May the new hand remember
And hold ever deeper
Your closeness and care,
The coal of Your love,
Till at long last all
Gloves are off and
I and You are One.

*BJ*

*In Need of a Street Corner*

Love fares no better in this world than
an unlicensed street peddler:
No sooner has he spread out his wares
at one street corner and seen
a handful of customers, than the authorities
appear and badger him to move on.
So what does he do?

He gathers his wares
and hurries on to another locality
and resumes his trade,
until he's harassed again.
Day in and day out, the same story.

Like an itinerant peddler,
love is not given a permanent street corner
in this world.
Even when love is given out for free,
as Jesus and Mohammed did centuries ago,
do you think they were ever allowed
to stay in any one place for long?
If I make one plea to you, it is
to always give accommodation to those
who are trying to love.

*JW*

*Short Story*

After the Lord visited its town, the Bogus News ran a story with this headline: "Master Thief Steals Multiple Hearts! Police Confounded!"

Sensing a deeper story behind the derisive laughter, one enterprising reporter decided to interview a devotee of the Lord, who happened to be a mast, and took these notes:

"Nowhere else to be
No more you or me
Nowhere else to go
No one else to know
No more if and then
No more why or when
Nothing left to do
But fly home to You"

The reporter submitted these notes while dancing naked on the editor's desk, then bolted laughing from the building never to return. The editor choked on the butt of his cigar.

Police remain confounded.

*BJ*

*Withdrawing the Tentacles?*

Where we put our consciousness
is of immense importance—
if we immerse it in thoughts,
we inherit a mind and we live from there;
if we entangle consciousness
in physical wants and desires,
we're saddled with a body
and now must protect it
and satisfy its appetites;
when it is enmeshed in the whole range
of emotions, we become heir to a personality
and enter the world of competition
and self-promotion.

Yet when consciousness
is wholly immersed in the Beloved,
we become divine.
Then, like breathing, all the functions
of body, mind and personality
are carried out automatically.
We become the ocean,
and all sea creatures and marine life,
the ceaseless movement of waves and currents,
joyously dance within us.

JW

*Sitting in the Corner*

Be still mind, be still.
You have nothing to add
To this conversation.
Your place is behind,
Your job observation.

Be still mind, be still.
You have no choice now.
Accept that your perception,
Comparison and judgment,
Are useless deflection.

Be still mind, be still.
Learn that all fear,
Imagining, grasping,
Are utterly useless.
Stop all this gnashing.

Be still mind, be still.
In this life for Him
You must follow.
You must obey.
No more leading,
Having your way.

Be still Bob, be still.

*BJ*

*A Piece of the Rock*

Today the Beloved is in the mood
to hand out free property deeds
to anyone willing to say goodbye
to all other places except
the land of this present moment.
Homestead this very moment long enough,
He assures us,
and we will inherit its vast acreage.

But this is no easy proposition.
To do this, we must not leave
the boundaries of this moment
for an instant--
no dwelling on the accomplishments
and sufferings of the past,
or on plans and fears
for the future.

This does not mean that
the past and the future can't be
thought of in the present—
only that consciousness must not be allowed
to project itself energetically beyond this moment.
There is a subtle difference.
Discover this secret, and our acreage
will increase a hundredfold.

But don't stop there, the Beloved says,
because hidden at the core of the present moment
is a secret passage into the eternal Now,
that timeless kingdom of the spirit,
where all beauty and loving abundance reside.
Go there just once,
and even the vast present will seem to us
like a tiny plot,
as insubstantial as the shadowy realms
of the imaginary future and the frozen past.

This glorious kingdom awaits us,
says the Beloved.
Are we ready to stake
our claim?

*JW*

*On the Road*

There is a certain slant of morning light
that sets the shadowed room aglow,
paints lace curtains shimmering on the wall,
and the red dog in the yellow chair shines
bright, a godly dog on a throne of light.

The sandstone canyons I long to walk,
portals to each infinitely ordinary moment—
canyons, neither the walls enclosing the gap
nor the bright blue gap itself, but radiance
conceived in the heart and the sun and born
just now upon red dog, red rock, hands
youthful again in this sanguine light—

Portals awaiting some simple incantation,
some slight shift, a different slant of gaze,
intention, awaiting, perhaps, Your grace,
Beloved, to pass through and transform,
become other than rubble of anticipation,
errant desire, fear, everything no longer
useful, yet hitched and loaded, traveling
endlessly like some impossible caravan.

As I rise resigned to time and distance,
passing clouds transform the lace
to mourning veils, then shrouds, and
all the mundane world crowds back;
lace becomes after all just curtains,
rusty dog sleeps in a battered chair,
canyons appear gray now and flat.

At last, after hours on this winding road
between necessity and You, just before
sunset a moment of sudden brilliance
glows and sings again in the heart.
Then last shadows fall in the fast falling light
till I lay me down silent in the long arms of night.

*BJ*

### A Few Miserly Drops

The Beloved once revealed that every moment
the infinite ocean of divine love crashes against
our soul, but by the time it passes through us,
what emerges is a mere rivulet, or at most a river.
Imagine that—every moment the ocean reduced
to a small stream! With His lively humor,
the Beloved illustrated this for me—

a man is seated in a chair, with powerful ocean
waves striking against him from behind.
In front, the man has his hand on a small spigot,
from which he offers this thirsty world only a few
miserly drops! What became of the stupendous
ocean, and why is so little offered to others?
Almost all of this abundant love is siphoned off
and used to protect and promote our self.

With saints and mystics, the divine ocean passes
through them with little obstruction.
That is how they can instantly fill a whole room,
a huge auditorium, or even an entire countryside,
with pure love.

*JW*

*Waiting at the Well*

November morning in the schoolyard,
Fingers peek like wary turtles from coat sleeves.
Sparrows tumble from cottonwoods,
A winged cataract swirling with the first flakes
And last desiccated remnants of leaves.
Children hurry at the bell,
And only the teacher would rather be out,
Listening to wind, rush of wings,
Rub and clack of naked branches,
Listening at the echoing well of his heart.

BJ

*Could It Be Otherwise?*

If the infinite knowledge,
power and bliss of God walked
through the streets of a great city,
how would it look,
clothed in human form?
Might He not appear sometimes
as helpless as the least of us,
His face full of sorrow and His walk unsteady
under the weight of this world?

Those who have seen Him
throughout the ages say that,
because of His unfailing compassion,
He often appears infinitely vulnerable,
a broken man,
forced to shuffle unsteadily
with all His strength to meet us—
all because of the resistance in our hearts
that keeps us from running forward
to meet Him and save God
that great effort.

*JW*

*Relative Distance*

Sitting in stalled traffic
listening to horns and shouts,
watching weary, angry faces,
this comes over the radio:
"The most distant object ever seen
in the sky is 12.3 billion light years away.
That places it 13 billion Years ago in time,
only 500 million or so from the Big Bang."
Between that and this stretches
time beyond naming, and we,
powerless to master, seek to blunt
time's sting by measuring.
Our Beloved explained that all war
is nothing more than the cresting
tide of all the private little angers
and hatreds we loose upon the world.
Not hard to believe where I sit
too close to a hundred shaking fists.
Perhaps, along with the airbag warning,
we need posted on every sun visor
a thought from Rumi who prayed
a few centuries ago as we measure time,
"Make us afraid of how we were."

BJ

*An Unseen Hand*

A puppet comes out on the stage
and proceeds to give a sermon
on free will:

"Don't let anyone tell you that you
don't have a choice in what you say or do.
You're all free souls like me,
free to decide the course
of your own life. Don't go on and on
tormenting yourself with questions like:
Is there really an unseen hand
behind all this?"

The audience howled with laughter.
But consider this, dear friend—
have you ever thought that maybe
the great mystics and the Divine Puppeteer
might be laughing to themselves at us
and all our talk about
living our own lives?

*JW*

*Into the Depths*

There are eyeless things
Armored in ocean depths
Rooted to lips of volcanic vents.
Twisting in dark, strange winds
They suck the searing gasses
Unaware of forces that feed them.
From that depth to this seems far.
And yet...

*BJ*

*Through a Glass Darkly*

Have you ever watched someone
through your window, and even waved to them,
but because of the reflection
they couldn't see you?

That's how the Beloved is with us,
following our every mood and feeling—
full of delight at our happiness
and hurt when we feel bad about ourselves—
and yet we often don't know He's there.

Why? Because we keep seeing
our own reflection in front of us.
But do this—step very close to the window
and look in, and you'll be eternally surprised
by the Beloved's warm adoring face.

JW

*Lost and Found*

Even now in early morning as You fill my heart,
Mind hints the day may darken, may not flower,
And all the clever fictions and broken parts
From that dark well will prove its darkest power.
I try to remember, repeat Your name
As day grows and mind reclaims its might,
And heart, abandoned to this weary game,
Must follow stumbling blindly into night.
Yet in this place where You have put me I remain,
For no imagined change can this thirst slake,
And from Your ocean wafts warm a hint of rain
As You build up and break as You will break.
Only where He wants you—stand that ground,
And there lose all but love till He is found.

BJ

*Caught Up in the Melodrama*

How could we all be God
with infinite consciousness,
as our Beloved maintains?
He explains by way of this analogy:
we're all sitting in a movie theater,
each identified with a different character
on the screen, so much so that
when our character triumphs, we triumph;
when our character fails, our spirits sink—
we get totally caught up in the drama.

But at the end of the movie,
as the credits roll
and the lights come up,
we will find ourselves in our seats,
with our half-eaten bag of popcorn
and empty soda cup.
Projecting our infinite consciousness
onto a finite drama,
we temporarily became someone we are not,
getting completely carried away
with our tiny part.
Do you think the Beloved, perhaps, is right?
Maybe, behind this vast drama of creation,
we all could be the one God!

JW

*Butterfly at October's End*

It is far too cold for you today.
Your brothers and sisters
Have long since fled, but here you are,
Far too bright for pale October,
Dancing above the skeletal garden.
Are you the same one my son saved,
The crooked one, unable to fly
Though he held you, offered flowers,
The sky? You? Dancing this fall light
Thin as dry marigolds,
Back for another try at awkward life,
Unable still to get it quite right?
Go now. It is seed time.
There is nothing I can do.
Today we share the failing light,
A bitter wind.
You will freeze, my friend,
But I am pinned.

*BJ*

*A Cruel Tailor*

Most of us go on stuffing our pockets
with the souvenirs of this world,
which we won't be able to take on to the next.
Their sheer weight makes it impossible in this life
to join in the thrilling dance of lovers of God.
We have to sit off to the side
and only witness their joy.
Even when we're invited to come out
on the dance floor, we hesitate—
where can we hang our heavy jacket that's safe?

The mystics laugh at our plight.
They know that on the day we die,
we'll be given a coat, tailored for the occasion,
that has no pockets!

*JW*

*New Year's Eve 1989*
   *After the Berlin Wall*

The wall is broken, mementos
Sold in chunks and shards.
And what of us in this new year?
Shall our walls, too, come down?
Who will take the broken pieces,
Hardened souvenirs of hurt?
Will we, too, rise up,
Walk out of smoking rubble
Into one another's embrace,
To attempt, at last,
Love?

*BJ*

*Could God Observe Such Protocol?*

Years ago, the Beloved once chided me:
"You say you are lonely
and feel cut off from others and the world.
But are you easily reached?
Are you one of those who has
a series of locked gates,
a sentry box and several guard dogs
that a visitor is confronted with
before he or she reaches the front entrance
to your heart's mansion?
And once inside,
do you hold your guest
to a strict protocol?"

I was like that, but the Beloved
got me drunk on love one night,
and in my intoxication,
I kicked open all the gates, threw out
the sentry and gave all my guard dogs
a year's supply of beef in the backyard.
In the presence of His love,
I lost all discrimination, and my heart
became a gathering place for thousands
of life's refugees.

I can still hear
the Beloved's admonishing words
ringing in my ears,
"Only one who wears his life on his sleeve
dares kiss the threshold of love,"
I who had always kept my heart
safely hidden behind my back
from others.

*JW*

*Nursery Rhyme*

As I was walking to St. Ives,
I met a man with 40 lives left.
He was, I think, a wandering mast
Who dressed in rags and ash and dust,
But hidden, had a treasure beyond price.
He cares for naught, but walks hard miles
For one of his Beloved's smiles,
Through storms we cannot see of fire and ice.
Dancing down the road he came
Singing Meher Baba's name,
And I enquired why he was not bereft.
I thought forty lives seemed very long
Even to mutter this wondrous song,
Much less sing joy on such a quest.

He laughed and took me by the hand,
Said "Child, let your heart expand.
If you'd any idea, if you only knew
How many lives we've all been through,
The endless ways we've been misled,
Waiting for a glimpse, the barest chance
To step along with the Lord of the Dance,
You could do forty standing on your head.
Oh the marvelous Lord of infinite Love
Who's everywhere below and above,
If you meet Him, catch his hem or eye
And ask Him please to drain you dry
Till you have nothing left to label 'mine.'

"Just limp along or run your race,
And beg the Lord to pour His grace
Until there's nothing left here to be seen.
Then you will finally come to know
All this is just a passing show,
You're finally awake, alive and free,
Lighter than air, immovable as stone."

I watched as he danced out of sight,
And knew I must somehow hold tight,
Remembering my Lord both night and day.
Whoever I am, whatever my song,
Whether this path be short or long
I will be Yours, Beloved, come what may.

BJ

*If You've Been Given a Dirty Cup*

The Beloved does not expect
our cup to be perfectly washed and dried
before He pours us His intoxicating wine.
Don't let the shame of your weaknesses
and impurities ever cause you
to hesitate to hold out a dirty cup
to the Beloved.

Our weaknesses and impurities
can awaken in us compassion,
which is the most precious gift
the Beloved bestows in this world.
What is compassion?
It is a love that is willing to kneel down
and share in the pain of others.
How is this possible if we have not known
their suffering?
One like St. Francis was even willing
to allow his heart
to be transformed into
another's pain,
and for that, he became
the beloved of our Beloved.

JW

*Homeland Security*

I am removing the plastic cone
From the old dog's head.
The young dog, always curious,
Makes the job difficult.
A friend knocks on the door;
Old dog jumps to her duty
And barks a ferocious alarm
Directly into my ear.
I leap before thought
And slap her on the rear,
Unmindful of tenderness there,
Anger damping down to regret
Not quite soon enough.
She yelps, jumps the young dog,
And my friend enters to shouting
And snarling and raising of fur.
I separate them, soothe, and though
Old dog cowers at first from my touch,
I whisper sorrow into silky ears,
Caress her drooping head,
Gaze into those eyes and see
What a tricky business it is
Searching for enemies outside.

BJ

## Seek the Real Fragrance

Most of us are explorers; we set out on
expeditions to find the beauty in this world—
a sunset over the ocean, millions of stars
on a clear winter night, a hidden meadow
of wildflowers, a newborn infant in its mother's
arms, an eagle in flight, a child's birthday party.
These are moments when the light-shafts of the
divine fall on our earth—a rare and fleeting beauty.
Throughout time, our Beloved has
insisted that there is a perennial source of beauty
that lies within us, a place from where beauty
itself is projected as if on a screen. That beauty is
so intoxicating that few can remain steady under
the influence of its ecstasy. The beauty on the
world's screen is only a shadow of a shadow of
that. It cannot give one that exquisite intimacy,
no more than a picture of a field of lavender
can impart to us its heady fragrance.

"Go inside," our Beloved says,
"I give My divine assurance
that within you lies the source
of all beauty you so desperately seek."

JW

*Dawn Remembered*

Mourning doves at dawn
Outside the summer window,
Their long delicious murmur
While dust gilt sun slants in,
Blooms on corners and edges,
Slants closer across the bed,
Blooms in his waiting hand
As the child lay somehow
Knowing, though not possessed
Of words, if he lay still enough,
That light, that joy might stay.

And what of this memory
Rising so clearly still in the
Cluttered mind of the man, rising
From somewhere deeper than memory,
Deeper than gristle and rushing blood
And all the beautiful connections
Attaching the body to itself,
The old longing rising,
The ache that knows no cause,
But knows.

*BJ*

*The Final Performance*

The Beloved explained,
"My being is the eternal stage
on which you play out
your fleeting melodramas.
When, at the end
of an exasperatingly long career,
you enact your final role,
casting aside costume and script,
you too become the eternal stage."

*JW*

*The Hangnail*

Nibble carefully at first
Leaving no ragged edge
To catch hotly the world,
Then gaining focus pull fiercely.
Ignore blood, drool, awkward
Set of jaw, small searing pain,
Then grip, tear from its mooring
The last intransigent flesh.
What, anyway, does this
Trembling finger own?

*BJ*

*Beyond Religion*

To Sufis, the path of religious observances
is called shariat, which is the word for a road,
one that is clear and well-marked. The inner path
is known as tariqat, which is the term
describing the route between two oases
in the desert—no roadway or signs
are visible. If you venture there, you must
either know the desert well or travel with a guide
who knows the way.

Choose a guide,
for as the great mystic Rumi says,
if you travel without a Master
it can take 200 years to make
a two-day journey.

*JW*

*Effort*

How does a man caught in quicksand
Find a safe place to stand?

No matter how he churns and thrashes
In this disaster he has not planned,

He is caught without hope, doomed,
Unless someone comes to lend a hand,

Someone who will reach with a stout
Stick from a safe place on solid land.

Does the mired one pause to assess he
Who holds the stick, who owns the hand,

Or to question the strength of the stick
Or the spot on which his helper stands?

Does he worry his clothes will be ruined,
Does he judge, compare, remember or plan?

No. He reaches, grabs and grasps the stick
With every ounce of strength he commands,

And he attends to the one holding the stick,
And does whatever that one demands.

Listen, Bob, this is the effort. Hold fast.
There is nothing else you need to understand.

BJ

*A Moment of Soul*

An encounter with our soul
is always dramatic, like stepping out
from a warm house full of rowdy friends
into a crisp cold winter night—
for a few moments you're alone
with your consciousness and the universe;
everything is seen in vivid detail,
your hazy mind assumes a great clarity,
and you know exactly where you're going.

Tell this to your friends and
they may just laugh.
They are yet to be surprised
by God on a snowy night,
when, in an ordinary moment,
consciousness is shattered
into a thousand brilliant lights,
like a silent snowfall
sparkling under a moonlit sky.

JW

*Dreaming the Music*

Alone under tattered canvas smelling
Of motor oil and fish and wood smoke,
The boy peered from the bed of the truck
Into the black blur of forest, snow, stars,
The moonstruck road unwinding behind.
When his face grew numb he pulled
The canvass tight and closed his eyes,
And the whistle of wind and long om of tires
Became melody, then harmony, then song,
A radiant choir singing grace in
Words he knew but did not understand,
And all he ever wanted was in that music,
And all he wanted was to go there and stay
In the light and song and be that music.
But some change in the road or rhythm of gears
Pulled him back, and though he shut tight
His eyes and wished as he had never before,
The choir faded and became again
Familiar humdrum of tires and wind.
The truck stopped and he climbed down.
Whatever it was he had heard was gone.
The boy said nothing to the men,
Because he could not then and he cannot
Now explain, and only the memory of music
He cannot hear remains.

*BJ*

*Typical Know-It-All*

Don't for a minute believe
in the conclusions handed down
to you by the ego-mind;
it specializes in making
the most dire predictions,
and a prediction when believed
too often becomes a self-fulfilling prophecy.
And when this happens,
the ego will whisper ever so condescendingly
in your ear, "See, I told you so!"

*JW*


Oh many-mirrored mind, you take my
deepest feeling, which is vast and whole,
and fracture it into a thousand
small and superficial pieces, claiming
that you have made a faithful translation.
But you have made something vast
into something very small; you've put the burning
of the soul into a mansion with many rooms,
but you've lost its warmth, its fire, its wholeness.

*JW*

*Afraid of the Cold*

Am I cut out for this?
Long ago, by Your grace, I made it
to the shore, but now after years
I see the disappointment on Your face
as I roll up my trousers
and wade into the cold surf.
I complain that I need time
to get used to the water,
and You keeping talking about
drowning!

*JW*


I find myself at the borderline between my deeper
heart and the timeless realm of the spirit where
You live in immensity, that place between the
physical and the intangible. You are inviting me to
cross over. Why do I hesitate? There are no
guards, no custom officials at the border crossing,
nothing before me to hold me back.
Your arms are outstretched.
For You there are no borders, no boundary lines.
You look surprised at my hesitation,
"Just fall into My arms, dearest one."

*JW*

*Head Lectures Heart*

What? You seek the path of Love?
Oh foolish, trustful heart, you've no defense.
Sit down here, have tea, listen to sense.
Why seek the tiger's lair? You're just a dove.
Yes, He has teased, given you a taste,
And now thirst grows and you want more,
But you don't know what you're asking for.
He will give you nothing but ruin and waste.
Best to plug your ears and run away.
Listen to me, listen, I'll do what I can
For your comfort, dear heart, I have a plan.
Come back where it's safe, I beg you, stay.
Oh fool, you're not in so far you can't turn back.
I'll untie His noose while there's still some slack.

*BJ*

*Heart Answers*

I have listened and followed you all my life,
Listened to all your fine dreams and designs,
But it's all about your needs, nothing of mine.
All you have brought is confusion and strife.
I know you too well and all of your tricks,
The fear and worry if I don't obey,
Your endless babble that darkens my day,
This cellar you've built of moldering bricks.
Listen: the best thing you can now do
Is remember Him and repeat His name,
Though it seems to you a tiresome game.
His wine is far better than your bitter brew.
You think I'm weak but in Him I'll grow strong,
And He'll teach you to help as you follow along.

*BJ*

*But What About Me?*

Great souls have gone before us,
who braved the terrible agony of defeat,
who climbed the sheer mountain of human
imagination, and losing their footing,
fell into the unspeakable chasm
of oblivion before descending into paradise.

All this I've heard about, listening in vivid detail.
I only laughed to myself at such graphic
depictions of the end game, never thinking that it
could be so unutterably harrowing,
but now I catch a glimpse of what is to come,
and I flee from such visions, preferring the
comfortable round of daily life surrounded
by close friends and observing the customary
devotions.

Naively, I am counting on
Your gentle intervention when the time comes.
And so I stay far, far from the goal--utter oblivion
in Your final embrace.

JW

*Climbing without Ropes*

Ragged, side by side long days they marched,
Or where the way was rough all in a line,
Not just bodies but their hearts were parched,
Wanting nothing but a sip of Your best wine.
At times they split up and struggled lonely
Through stinking, arid cities boiling in strife,
But always came together knowing only
With You dwells truth and love and life.
And here we are, Your scattered band of lovers,
Spread out on the longest trail there is to tread
Seeking a vintage surpassing all the others,
Your company here, not somewhere up ahead.
Unless You pour all drink is bitter dregs,
And all this talk of marching won't grow legs.

*BJ*

*A Divine Bargain*

On the scales of divine grace,
for one seed, You give us
a meadow of wildflowers;
for one sin given, a hundred virtues;
for one sincere prayer, days of well-being.

My face flushes with warmth,
as Your grace dissolves into
this gratefulness I feel.

*JW*

*Walking to the Store*

This world expands to cloudless blue,
and day breathes perfect air for strolling through.
Lean close and look, listen to tribes of bees

working mint and Russian sage and the few
remaining milkweed blossoms, heavy now
and dry in this world expanding to endless blue.

There is no how or why as heart expands too,
greets the old man by the pond, those waiting
for the bus, and the grocery store crew,

and then returning, not the quiet way I always do
but by the busy street as traffic swoops and skates
and workers small as bees bustle over the new

apartment tower growing into that endless blue,
and people come and go and take and give
and there is nothing of sadness, nothing of rue.

If I could stay I'd never leave this bottomless blue.
I'd rather walk this than any other way,
this perfect day my Lord, for strolling with You.

BJ

*This is a Bargain!*

A saint once told me:
The personality is just
a storefront for the soul.
You make so much of the window displays,
changing them with the seasons.
Be bold and
step through the door and claim
aisle upon aisle
of priceless merchandise within,
manufactured in the factories
of Paradise.

*JW*

*Shopping for Shoes*

Ties, watches, alluring colognes all on sale,
and clothing of soft cotton, cashmere and silk.
I would wear them if they enticed Your notice.

Cookware and kitchen tools to help prepare
delicious meals, but nowhere the book
of recipes that would bring You to my table.

The finest handcrafted Italian luggage
I would gladly buy if I could pack away
all my cherished obstacles to Your love.

As to shoes, nothing seems to fit,
but I would limp in any awkward pair
that might help me walk toward You.

Outside, there are rows of shiny new cars.
I would sell everything to buy the one
that could speed me to Your door, Beloved.

Mind spins and heart aches with not wanting
these things; you accept that He is everywhere,
but only His grace will let you finally meet
Him there.

BJ

*His Tomb*

My house is overrun with junk;
in the attic, the accumulation of trunks
of memorabilia, knickknacks,
things I thought I might have
a use for at some time;
the basement full of old books
I'll never read again,
old manuscripts in the hallways,
books of designs and plans for the future,
other people's stuff they've stored with me,
dog leavings, furniture losing its stuffing,
two and three of everything–
and then one morning I wake up
and how extraordinarily fortuitous!
Someone has backed a huge garbage truck
right up to the front of the house,
the back-end opening perfectly level
with the porch steps,
and I begin unloading all this mess;
in fact, I go insane throwing things out,
back and forth and heave ho!
Not sorting through anything,
not looking back, not dreaming ahead,
and what do they call this
great unsentimental junk remover?
His tomb!

*JW*

*Dhuni*

Beloved Lord, I surrender all resistance
That this distance between us may go.
Yes, I know, such surrender still courts desire,
But from this desert it's my only chance.
I cannot sing or dance, but I offer these scraps
Just so You know how my heart cries out.

Oh Bob, you have no charm, no potion,
No magical motion, no right to insist.
Beg then, from this arid headland,
For a breath, a taste of His ocean.

*BJ*

*An Incredible Stretch*

You're sitting around with friends,
playing music together and singing,
when someone comes along
and picks up a drum and joins in.
But that person can't keep a beat.
So what do you do?
Adjust.

You make the human adjustment,
playing to the weak link and find a way
to make a new music, until gradually
the person finds the rhythm.
For a time, the music suffers,
but eventually it becomes acceptable,
maybe even beautiful
if you're lucky.

That's what happens when new people
come into our circle—
we stretch.
Just consider how far our Beloved
has had to stretch
for each of us.

*JW*

*Jacob's Ladder*

Here, at the end of the Kali Yuga,
we have heard of a time long ago
when Jacob stopped for the night,
placed a stone under his head
and dreamed of angels going up
and coming down a stairway.
This ancient image so brilliant
the words are stuck to anything,
anywhere the imagination can go,
Jacob's ladder this thing and that
from old hymns and quilt patterns
to festivals and games and gardens.
Pete Seeger may have been closer
when he sang "We are climbing
Jacob's ladder, brothers, sisters all."
Nothing of damnation or exclusion,
only the eternal going and coming
together, and perhaps the final climb
back to You, Beloved Lord.

*BJ*

*The Destination is Not on the Map*

There are those who study their own scriptures
and even become great authorities,
expounding on the meaning of this passage,
or quibbling over the wording of that text.
And they don't stop there; they will even argue
with people from other religions over the truth
of their scriptures.

They don't see that the scriptures of all the world
religions are mere road maps—memorizing the
best routes to take, and quarrelling with others
about their choice of travel, will not take them
a single step on the spiritual path.

What is needed is to pack a few things,
climb in our own vehicle, and set out
for the destination. To have a perfect map
is not necessary before starting out—
do you think our Beloved would be upset
by any inaccuracies on our road map?

Just set out—how can anyone be content
like some scholars with a mere map of the
journey, when our ultimate destiny is
to stand and breathe in the rarified
atmosphere of the Beloved Himself?

JW

*"You Go"*

Our Beloved Lord, during His visit here,
Explained so many wonderful things.

I have read and read so much,
Yet still forgot that in silence He sings.

Whose company I long for most?
He alone who gives this heart wings.

Oh Bob, just set out, just go;
Cast off all that confuses and clings.

Simply love Him however you can;
Seek to be His, whatever that brings.

*BJ*

*Bird's Eye View*

For You, Beloved, life is like
a view of the earth from the air,
a broad flat patchwork of enchanting
and gloriously colorful design—
a creation of unimaginable beauty.
But do you give a thought to us
down here?

For us, life is mostly
the agonizing ups and downs
of a rough terrain, a few coarse brushstrokes
in one small corner
of an artist's vast landscape painting—
Your masterpiece.
How are we to appreciate its beauty
without some higher viewpoint?

Your answer is—
throw off the weight
of heavy desires and wants that keep you
earthbound,
and naturally in time you will rise
to this undreamed-of height,
where exquisite beauty is seen
everywhere.

*JW*

## The King's Falcon

> *after "The King's Falcon Is Your Soul"*
> *pastel by Nancy Bohm*

Hooded in darkness,
Entranced by Your scent
And the sound of Your flute,
She longs for a glimpse,
Perhaps a caress?
You, Beloved, counsel patience:
Obey me, and if you are
Fortunate, you will please me.
You are mine, and in time,
When I wish it, you shall fly.

BJ

## ABOUT THE AUTHORS

Jeff first heard of Meher Baba in the late 1960s during college in New York City and was immediately caught in His love net. Later he lived in Schenectady NY and attended Darwin and Jeanne Shaw's Baba meetings. In 1972, he moved to Myrtle Beach where he has been a caretaker at the Meher Center since 1977. Besides his daily duties, he has enjoyed singing, gardening, playing with the kids and meeting Baba's many wonderful guests who come to the Center.

Bob heard of Meher Baba in the late 1960's when a friend returned from India and handed him a copy of *The Everything and the Nothing*. Many questions were laid mercifully to rest, but it was on his first trip to India in 1976 that Beloved Baba captured his heart. Bob and his dear wife, Gerri, live near Denver, Colorado where they enjoy reading, quilting, gardening, good mysteries on TV, and the company of children, grandchildren, friends and fellow Baba folk.

Jeff and Bob have run into each other over the years at the Meher Center and in India. They have enjoyed each other's poetry and, too long ago to remember exactly when, hatched the idea of this combined volume. They hope it has brought pleasure, including a few chuckles.